RISE
Again

A GUIDE FOR RESILIENT WOMEN IN CHAOTIC TIMES

NINA MADSEN

Special Art Development

Rise Again

A Guide for Resilient Women in Chaotic Times

Paperback ISBN: 979-12-5553-002-2
support@specialartbooks.com
www.specialartbooks.com

© Copyright 2023 — Nina Madsen, Special Art

It is not legal to reproduce, duplicate, or transmit any part of this document in either electronic means or in printed format. Recording of this publication is strictly prohibited and any storage of this document is not allowed unless with written permission from the publisher except for the use of brief quotations in a book review.

Table of Contents

Introduction 5

Part 1: Love Your Generosity 7

Chapter One
    Embrace Mindfulness with Your Device 8

Chapter Two
    Love Being On Your Own 13

Chapter Three
    Develop Your Courage 17

Chapter Four
    Give Yourself a Gift 23

Part Two: Love Your Buoyancy 28

Chapter Five
    Indulge in Rest 29

Chapter Six
    Build Up Your Knowledge 34

Chapter Seven
    Create Confidence 39

Chapter Eight
    Reflect on Your Progress 44

Part Three: Love Your Truth 49

Chapter Nine
    Guard Your Boundaries 50

Chapter Ten
  Always Be Prepared 55
Chapter Eleven
  Be Your Own Workout Buddy 59
Chapter Twelve
  Let Go of Negativity 64

Part Four: Love Your Capacity to Grow 68

Chapter Thirteen
  Indulge in Meditation 69
Chapter Fourteen
  Grow an Incredible Garden 73
Chapter Fifteen
  Fight the Good Fight 78
Chapter Sixteen
  Inspire Yourself With Words 82

Part Five: Love Your Power 86

Chapter Seventeen
  Anchor Yourself 87
Chapter Eighteen
  Love Your Look 91
Chapter Nineteen
  List Your Strengths 95
Chapter Twenty
  Give Yourself More Physical Space 100

Final Words 104

Introduction

Resilience–this is a popular term right now, and it's a good thing too. Finally, people are talking about resilience, the ability to bounce back from difficulty, and how to develop it in their lives. The common teaching is that to have a good life, you should be kind, hardworking, and find someone you love.

However, the development of resilience is often overlooked. Resilience is tapping into that inner strength that everyone possesses. It's about believing that you have the courage and the ability to muscle through difficult times and come out on the other side still standing.

There will be a lot of battles in your life. Battles such as arguments with loved ones, the death of a family member, getting fired, losing money, or even getting a divorce. Everyone has their own burdens to bear as they move through their lives.

But what makes the biggest differences are those who have resilience and know how to put it into practice.

You have that potential already within you. All you need to know is how to build it and access it. In this book, I want to show you how you can work on your resilience through self-love and attention, building up your courage, strength, and determination.

Build resilience through loving your generosity, loving your buoyancy, loving your truth, loving your capacity to grow, and finally, loving your power. Even if we have loved ones surrounding us in the day-to-day, we still need to be able to depend on ourselves.

It is us who get through difficult times, and no one else can do that for you. Take the burden upon your shoulders; take responsibility for yourself and your life, and be proud and resilient. Life and its whims do not have to control you. Instead, resilience makes it possible for you to take control of your life and see all the good things about it.

Part 1: Love Your Generosity

Chapter One

Embrace Mindfulness with Your Device

> *It's all about falling in love with yourself and sharing that love with someone who appreciates you, rather than looking for love to compensate for a self-love deficit.*
>
> —Eartha Kitt

It isn't really possible to get away from technology these days, especially social media. Our phones have become linked to our bodies, and sometimes our jobs. There are literally job titles of people who focus solely on developing a company's social media. So, there's no real getting away from it all. But a break might be just the thing to get you out of a funk in your life.

Social media has totally spurred on an epidemic of mindlessness. Just think, we are always scrolling, looking at content constantly, and it takes no thought. We sort of get lost in a weird haze with social media. For some, it can be relaxing, like television, because it's a time of no stress and no thinking.

But unfortunately, too many mindless activities can really put us into a sort of depressive state. Our minds aren't engaged, and thus we lose track of the present. Then when tough times come along, we just don't have the resilience to get through it effectively. However, if you practice good habits with your device, you can embrace mindfulness in other areas of your life too.

Put It into Practice

There are certainly benefits to using social media, but scrolling endlessly can leave you feeling totally depleted. It's a mindless activity that doesn't actually bring any energy or zest to your life. Rather than mindlessly using social media or scrolling through news sites predicting doom, aim to change your relationship with your phone and other devices. Embrace mindfulness.

Look for apps that feature time alerts, shut-down options, or that block certain features like a timeline to help you become more mindful about your screen time. Once you get your screen time down, find other ways to occupy yourself—read a book, sit quietly, go for a walk outside, visit a neighbor. Show yourself that your downtime can be valuable and not something to just use up.

Then, when you go back to your device, think about what you look at and why. See if you can find five or six accounts that genuinely inspire you when you spend time online. Look for artists, performers, writers, maybe even a guided meditation. Make your screen time more valuable.

CREATIVE EXERCISE

Sketch a picture of a peaceful outdoor setting, like a beach chair by the ocean or a park bench next to a beautiful lake. As you draw, remind yourself that relaxation, quiet, and nature awaits you if you live with intention.

Conclusion

Start being mindful about your time, what you see, and what you put into your head. When you are mindful, you are enjoying the present moment. You're not just enduring it and scrolling through content to avoid thinking about other things. Enjoy the present moment and build up your resilience to make you stronger than ever.

Chapter Two

Love Being On Your Own

> Never bend your head.
> Always hold it high.
> —*Helen Keller*

The road to loving ourselves can be a long journey. While it's sometimes easy to forgive others for their wrongdoings, it can be a massively difficult thing to forgive yourself or just give yourself a break every now and then. One of the ways you can do that is to love your own company and love being on your own when the opportunity presents itself.

If you don't yet love being on your own, it's time to think about why. What stops you from taking the time to enjoy the silence? Is it really about not having enough time, or is there something deeper that prevents you from finding stillness?

Taking time for yourself will look different for every person. Just be mindful that the time should be in a place you feel safe or doing an activity you love.

Put it into Practice

One thing I would recommend is to create a space in your house that's solely for you. This could be a study, a reading nook, or even just a special chair. Whatever you do with yourself in this space is up to you, but it's a place in the world where you can go to be alone, to think your own thoughts without judgment, and do something that brings you happiness.

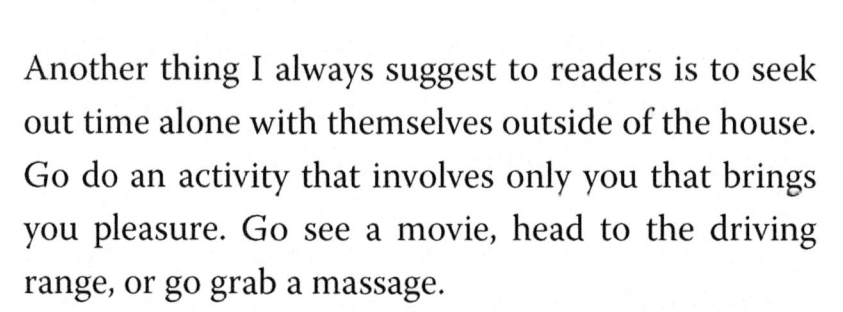

Another thing I always suggest to readers is to seek out time alone with themselves outside of the house. Go do an activity that involves only you that brings you pleasure. Go see a movie, head to the driving range, or go grab a massage.

CREATIVE EXERCISE

Draw an image of yourself sitting alone in a comfortable chair and thinking. Your figure in the drawing should look happy and at peace. Alone time shouldn't be stressful. It should be a place of escape. Return to this image when you're unsure about finding more alone time.

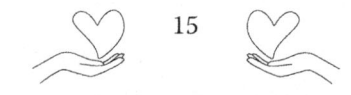

Conclusion

Loving yourself and connecting with yourself involves spending time on your own. Just like anything, the more you do it, the better you become at enjoying alone time and taking benefits away from it. Also, as you build up that confidence in and love of yourself through alone time, you will also be able to build up your resilience.

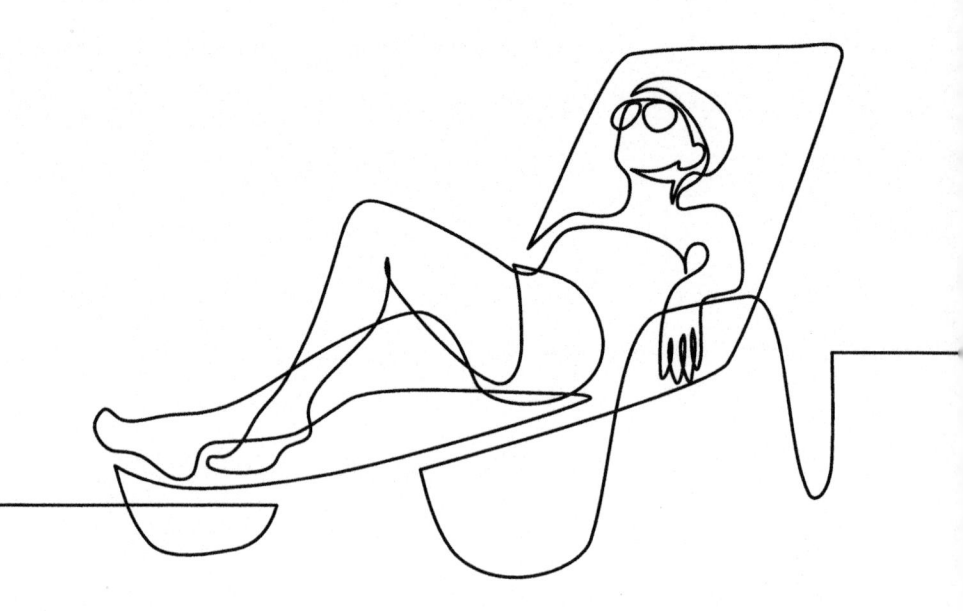

Chapter Three

Develop Your Courage

> Do one thing every day that scares you.
> —*Eleanor Roosevelt*

A lot of people think that having courage means you aren't afraid. We read adventure stories and watch exciting movies where the main characters are always so bold. They don't seem afraid as they jump into fighting a dangerous foe or exploring a mysterious area. Then, we might think, oh, I could never do that. I'd be too scared! But that's actually not the way we should think of courage.

Courage is the decision to do something even though it scares you. It may leave you shaking, but taking that step into what you're afraid of can really help you grow as a person. Fear doesn't control us, and we can still achieve goals and make progress, despite our fear.

Pushing past our fear is exactly what builds our resilience. If we always give in to our fears and allow them to keep us away from doing what we need to, then we get used to hiding. So, when difficult times in our lives come, then we just hide and maybe don't deal with the difficulty. But the more practiced you are at facing your fears and doing what you're afraid of, the better you'll be in those hard times. You'll be powerful and resilient, even if you go numb with terror in the process.

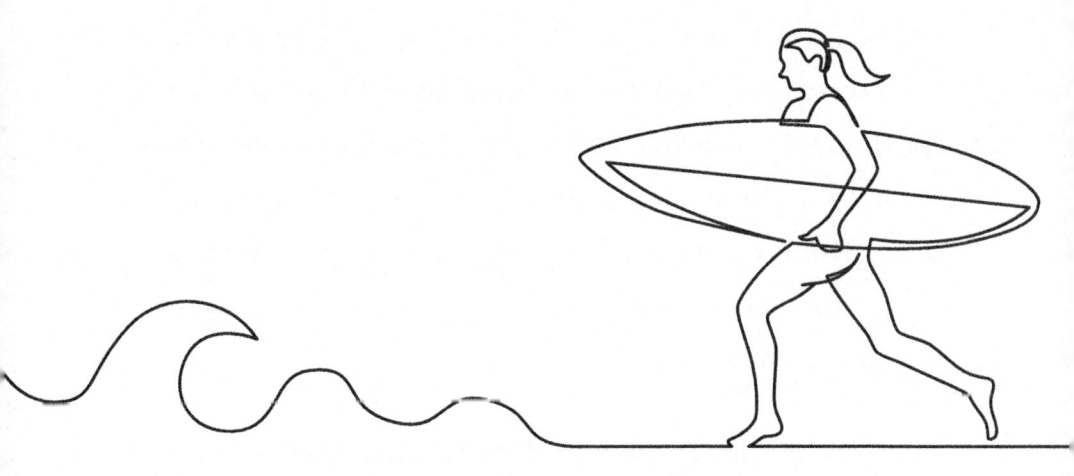

PUT IT INTO PRACTICE

Eleanor Roosevelt's famous words can act as your mantra. Do one thing a day that scares you. It should become a routine and a habit just like eating fruits and vegetables every day. Take out your journal and start listing out things that scare you, especially things you would love to be able to do or know you need to. If you're looking for ideas, just go through the list to spot a few of your fears.

Are you afraid of:

- rock climbing?
- public speaking?
- meeting new people?
- asking for a promotion?
- asking someone out?

Whatever it is, write it down. Start to explore that fear. What is the worst that could happen if you tried one of these fears? Write down a few truly terrible scenarios if you were to approach a stranger, for instance.

....

....

....

....

....

Once you've identified these worst-case scenarios, then contact someone who's done one of your fears before. Ask them to share their experience, how they got through it, as well as what they learned from doing something like this.

After that, pick one of your fears and make the decision to try it. Be sure to give yourself permission to do it badly or to fail completely. That's ok. Remember what the other person said about what they learned from working through their fears.

Creative Exercise

Illustrate an image that leaves you in awe. It could be a mountaintop, someone speaking in public, or a scene of courage and bravery, whatever it might be. Picture yourself in the setting as you sketch it. Remember that fear is only natural, but it doesn't have to hold you back.

Conclusion

Doing things that scare you may not sound all that fun, but you might surprise yourself at how much you enjoyed something you feared. Or if you didn't enjoy it, you still will have learned something. Goodbye fear; hello resilience!

Chapter Four

Give Yourself a Gift

> Self-care is how you take your power back.
> —Lalah Delia

At Christmas, we'll make a long list of everyone we have to get a gift for, and we'll put a gift idea next to their name. But the person who is hardly ever on your own gift-giving list is yourself! Why do people think so often of giving gifts to others, but they neglect to remember themselves?

Don't go overboard, stay within your budget and be realistic about space. At the same time, keep in mind that there is so much to be gained when you start giving gifts to yourself. It's a way to remind yourself that even though the world can be a cruel, wild place, you still deserve love, respect, and attention. You're worth a gift, and sometimes, you just need to be told that, even by yourself!

Put it into Practice

Think about what you love and what would make you happy to receive as a gift. I often encourage people to consider a spa day. Not only is it time with yourself, but it's also luxurious and totally focused on you and your enjoyment. Get yourself a spa gift card for future use. Then, when the time comes, it will feel super special when you decide what day you're free for a day of relaxation.

Also, start stockpiling little gift cards here and there to use for a rainy day when you really need to gift yourself a little something. You can purchase a little gift card each time you check out at most stores. Save them up, and then voila! You've got a little pile of cash totally dedicated to providing you with a wonderful gift.

Give Yourself a Gift

You don't need an excuse to give yourself a present, but one way you can use these little gifts are as rewards for achieving goals you've set for yourself. Let's say you decided to try something that scared you. Give yourself a gift as a way to pat yourself on the back!

CREATIVE EXERCISE

Create an image of something you'd like as a gift. Go beyond material things and consider something you would love to receive as a gift, something that has meaning for you. It can be something you are working towards as you slowly get into the practice of giving yourself gifts.

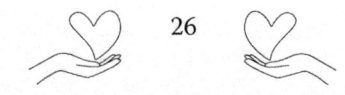

Conclusion

Don't leave yourself off the Christmas list this year or any gift-giving list. Not that you actually have to give yourself a Christmas present, but start thinking of yourself as someone worthy of gifts and attention. Gifts are a beautiful love language, and when you give yourself a gift, you're showing to yourself, "Hey, you matter."

Part Two: Love Your Buoyancy

Chapter Five

Indulge in Rest

> "Self-care is not about self-indulgence.
> It's about self-preservation.
> —Audre Lorde"

Ah, rest. Even the word contains a sound and a feeling of letting go, of complete relaxation. Animals and humans both spend time at work and rest. It's just the way of things, but as time went on, we began to focus more on the work than the rest. Rest has fallen by the wayside so much in many people's lives that insomnia, burnout, and the drive to overwork have become rampant.

Rest sounds decadent. It sounds luxurious, and for some, it may sound selfish. Sleep is utilitarian. We all sleep, and physically our bodies require it, but rest is something different entirely. Rest is a focus on slowing down, letting your body and your mind pump the brakes a bit. Sleeping is part of rest, but there are so many other ways you can find rest in your life, to give yourself a little break.

Meditation, napping, daydreaming, and just sitting in quiet are some of the ways you can indulge in beautiful and restorative rest. In rest, you are not conscious of the passing of time nor are you worried about it. You are simply being and allowing yourself the space and the permission to take a breath.

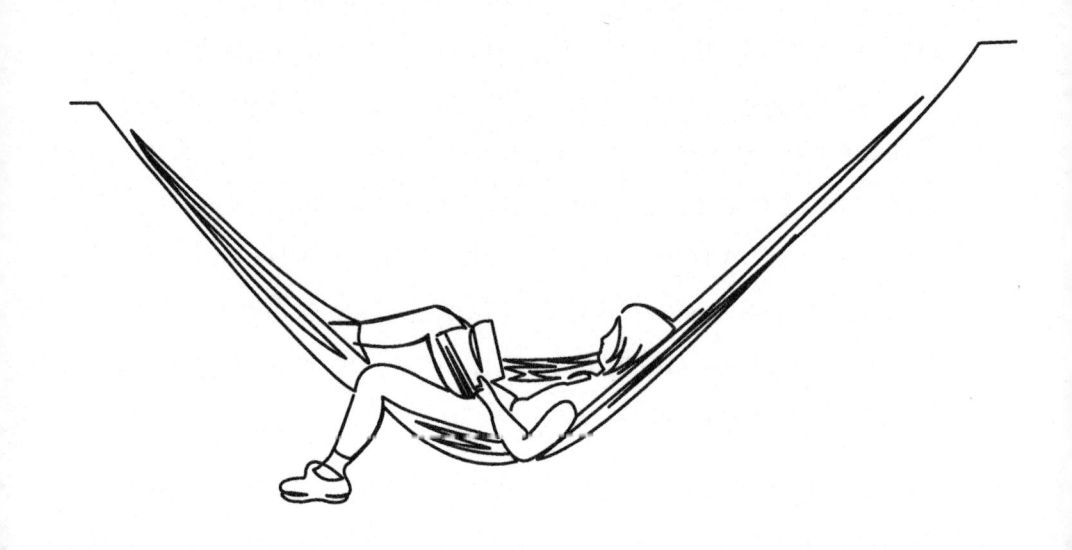

PUT IT INTO PRACTICE

First of all, sleeping is part of rest, so let's start there to make it simple. To get into the right headspace, reevaluate your bedroom space. A lot of times, we bring so many other things into our bedroom, like devices or workout equipment even though that space should be kept sacred for sleep and for rest. Look around your room. Is everything in there devoted to rest and sleep?

For example, bring things into the room that remind you of peace and rest. Suggestions are things like a beautiful seashell you found, a picture of a natural scene you took, or a few sprigs of rosemary from your herb garden. Decorate your room so that every night when you go into it, it feels safe, peaceful, and beautiful. Then, when you awake, your mind is still on peace and beauty as you start your day.

To help encourage better sleep, build up a routine that gets your body in the mood for rest at night. That way, you can sleep easily, and when you wake you are rested.

Now, let's focus on rest aside from sleep in your life. Rest is not sleep, but it's about taking a little time to just pump the brakes and take a step back. Rest is proven to help you with things like memory consolidation (Tucker, et al., 2020). But it's more than that. It's giving you a break without you having to actually go to bed for a full eight hours to get it.

I challenge you to carve out about two minutes a day devoted entirely to rest. Start at two minutes, and then see if you can work up to five or more. Find a quiet spot, and just sit there. Sit in your deck chair, your reading nook, or your hammock. Take a few calming breaths and enjoy the moments as you sit with them.

Creative Exercise

On a separate piece of paper, draw an image of rest: a soft bed, a sunrise, a hammock. Find something that brings the idea of 'rest' to your mind. Keep this image in view so that you are always reminded to take time to rest in your life. To pause and enjoy moments of true rest.

Conclusion

Even though it doesn't feel like it, there are still hours in the day in which to squeeze in some rest. Not counting getting a good night's sleep, focus on finding a few minutes here and there to take a pause and to just think about rest. Let your mind and body relax as you enjoy and savor that relaxation. You will find you have even more energy to do the things you love to do and to remain buoyant. The more rested and buoyant you are, the more your resilience will grow.

Chapter Six

Build Up Your Knowledge

> Knowledge has a beginning but no end.
>
> —Geeta Iyengar

Who says learning has to just happen in school? Even though you might not realize it, we are always acquiring new skills. How else can we learn to get through difficult times, change jobs, or even become a parent? Our minds are naturally curious, so, go out and seek opportunities for more knowledge.

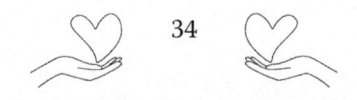

When you're learning something you're interested in you're not only exercising your brain but building confidence. Knowledge truly is power. You show yourself that you have the ability to gain new and interesting skills and information whenever you gain a new skill or new understanding.

Building up your knowledge also gives you the chance to explore some unique topics you might never have had the chance to explore before. And that just makes life all the more fun!

PUT IT INTO PRACTICE

Make a list of three topics that interest you. Is it the Civil War, physics, or British Literature? Once you've got your list, take steps to find opportunities to learn more about these topics. Can you find a book about them in the library? Is there a free class somewhere in your area? Maybe there's an online course you can take. Reading and learning are both empowering, and reading especially is a terrific way to practice mindfulness.

....

....

....

You're completely in the present as you research your topics and gain new knowledge. Nothing else matters, and you've given yourself the space to learn something new that interests you. What's more; reading, rather than watching a video, boosts cognitive function and boosts memory. After you learn more about something, find other people who love it as much as you do and get together with them to sit and discuss your new topic.

Build Up Your Knowledge

CREATIVE EXERCISE

Get an image (or create one) of a bookshelf so you can see all the book titles about your new topic. Color it as you think about all the knowledge that's out there for you. It's an endless journey, and that's the most exciting part. You can always, always, always learn more.

Conclusion

Learning boosts your brain, and at the same time, it gets you out of the same old funk. We can get so into our day-to-day drudgery and schedules that we forget to do other things. Our brain goes on autopilot. But with learning, you can expand your mind, and give yourself a fresh new perspective on life. Whenever you master new knowledge, the world around you opens up just a little bit more.

Chapter Seven

Create Confidence

> " I say if I'm beautiful. I say if I'm strong. You will not determine my story.
>
> —Amy Schumer "

So many of one's emotional issues come down to one thing: confidence and lack thereof. As we grow up, we're told what to be. We figure out how to walk, talk, and act, we try to look at everyone around us and fit in as best we can. It's only natural, and all the messages we receive tell us to be that way.

Fit in, don't stand out, look this or that way, only believe these things, the list goes on and on. Often, a lot of our confidence as women comes from our bodies. The world puts such a focus on women's bodies and how they're supposed to look, that it damages our whole self-confidence if we don't feel like we measure up.

But I challenge you to start building your own confidence. Stop waiting for other people to tell you that you deserve to be confident in yourself or that somehow you're worthy of finally having confidence. Just like anything else, confidence comes from within you. You decide your story; you decide how you feel about yourself. Don't let anyone else tell you how confident you should be.

Put it into Practice

Stand in front of a full-length mirror and observe yourself. In your journal, list out five aspects of your appearance that bother you or that you don't feel measure up to society's standard. Then, turn all these complaints on their head.

For example, if your wrinkles bother you, write down what your wrinkles say about you. How you love to laugh, be in the sun, and just enjoy life. If you don't love your legs, think about all the things you've been able to do with your legs over the course of your life – dance, hike, walk from one place to another.

The point of this exercise is not to pick out your flaws and work to change not your physical body but how you see it. It's about finding what you don't like and learning to love it. Learning to appreciate our bodies and accept them is all a part of how we can love ourselves as a whole. How can you show an appreciation to your physical body instead of just thinking of it negatively?

Maybe you want to give your legs a deep massage, thanking them for all they've given to you. Perhaps you want to go for a facial, giving back to the skin that has been with you all this time. Find ways to say thanks and focus on gratitude instead of negativity. Build your resilience. When you love your body and appreciate what it's given to you, the stronger you are inside and out.

CREATIVE EXERCISE

Draw an outline of your body, and remember to be kind to yourself! Look for ways to show your uniqueness and the parts of your body that tell a story. The wrinkles around your mouth show how much you smile and laugh. The piercing scar on your belly button shows your youth and rebellion. You could go on and on. Your physical body is all uniquely you. It's not everything you are, but it's a major part of you, and it should be loved and respected.

Conclusion

Be kind to yourself! It's a tad easier to be kind to ourselves about our less tangible and visible abilities. However, for women, it's tough to be kind to our physical bodies. We often just echo the voices of society, telling us how we're too fat or too thin, or too old. Learn to accept who you are and appreciate the body you have, instead of only focusing on what you don't have.

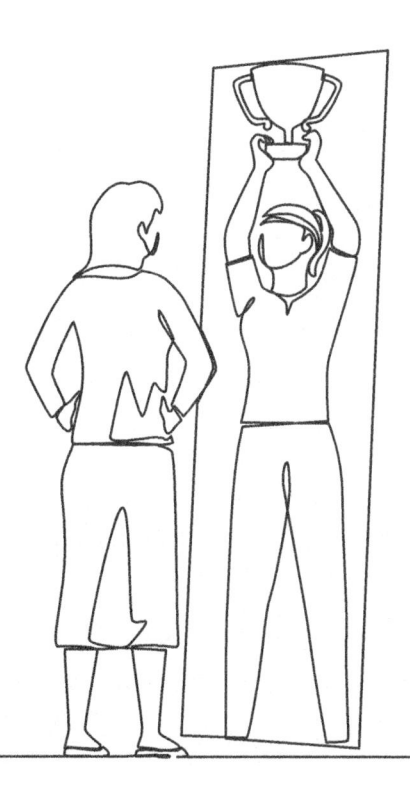

Chapter Eight

Reflect on Your Progress

> "Life is energy; pure creative energy.
> —Julia Cameron"

How can progress be noted if we don't actually sit down and think about how far we've come? Just like in school, you received grades and comments on your assignments to help guide you as to how you're doing. Now, I'm not saying that you need to grade yourself on your life skills and growth, but start thinking a little bit more about your progress and improvement.

It should be noted that the focus should not be on the end goal but on the journey. It's all about the journey, as they say, and too often we only think about getting to the end. Then, we miss all the important stuff along the way.

Reflecting on your progress is one way to focus on the positive and let the negative fade away into the background. It's saying to ourselves, "hey, look how much better you did this time," instead of "oh, you messed up again."

When you start to look at life this way, you can begin to put aside those fears that you don't measure up or that you'll never achieve the goals you always dreamed of. Progress is the new goal. Constant improvement and change is the new dream. If you improve, you're progressing, and that's a positive.

PUT IT INTO PRACTICE

Before bed, take out your journal and start writing with a focus on progress. Think about all areas of your life from work to family, and think about what things you learned that day or what improvements you've made in the past few weeks. Maybe you started standing up for yourself in a meeting. Or you signed up for an online class.

Even if it's not something as big as that but smaller such as, you realized something new about yourself that you need to work on, that's ok. Write it down. Show the progress you're making as you keep working towards becoming a happier, better you.

....

....

....

....

....

CREATIVE EXERCISE

Draw an image of a sunrise. We don't only think of the sun when it's at its height, shining down on us. We enjoy the sun in all states of its movement, from the pink, warming sunrise to the soft orangey sunset. It's the same with you. Wherever you are on your journey, you're there, and you're making progress.

Conclusion

Progress is the focus; improvement is the focus. Everyone and anyone can improve and get closer to their goals by putting in the effort to do so. But it's not about the end goal. It is all about that journey.

Part Three: Love Your Truth

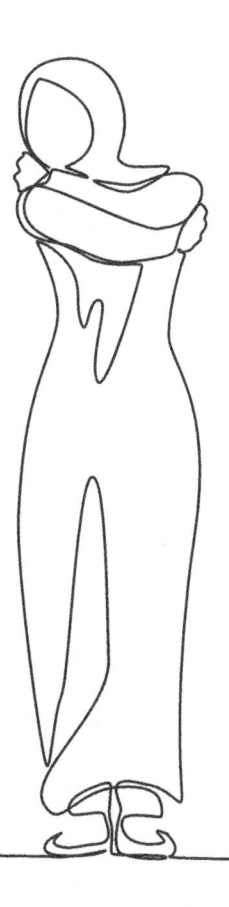

Chapter Nine

Guard Your Boundaries

> " As you grow older, you will discover that you have two hands: One for helping yourself, the other for helping others.
> —*Maya Angelou* "

Boundaries are so important, and it's shocking how little they're discussed. I grew up never learning a thing about boundaries, then had to manage them later in life. Part of loving yourself and building resilience against the vagaries of life is to build boundaries and guard yourself.

Boundaries are a way to protect yourself and show others that you will not allow them to just treat you however they wish. You need to say what you need and what you want if you expect anything from anyone.

One of the most important rules about boundaries is this: You cannot control the actions of others. You can only control yourself. Let me repeat that: You cannot control the actions of others. You can only control what you do and say. It's a little hard to swallow, but that fact can set you free.

When we realize that we have control over ourselves, we can take that control, and we no longer have to worry about anyone else. That's their business. What you need to do is discover where your lines are and how you can build them and guard them with both others and yourself.

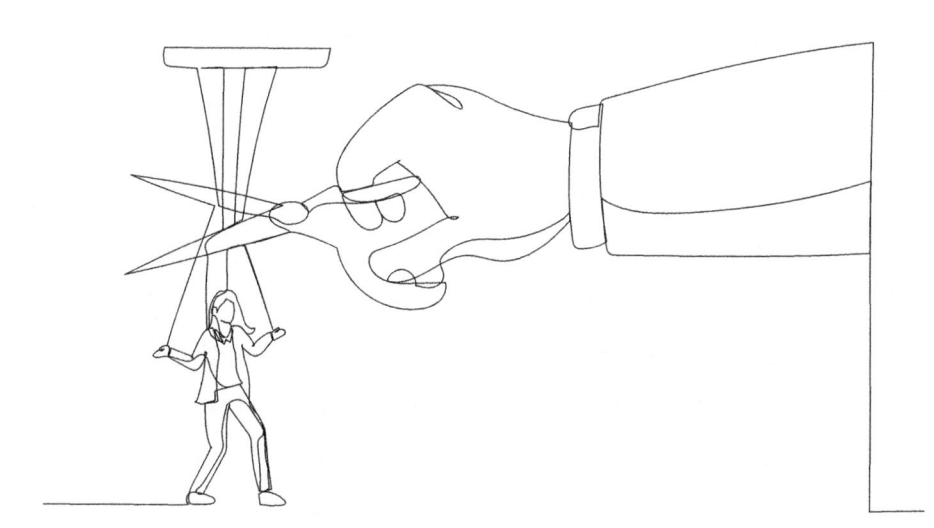

PUT IT INTO PRACTICE

To help you discover where your boundaries are, write down three things that trigger you. For example, let's say it's your sister texting you at 3 a.m., demanding an instant response. Maybe your neighbor starts weed-whacking at dawn. Or maybe it's news sites that leave you depressed.

Write down your triggers and start to think of ways you can build a boundary to protect yourself from them. For the sister issue, you can speak to her, or you can just put your phone on silent during the night. For the neighbor, why not speak to them and present a new solution? As for the news sites, maybe limit yourself to looking at them only once every few days or once a week so that you don't spend hours doom-scrolling.

Remember, not everyone will respond well to your boundaries. Your neighbor might still rise before the sun to terrorize his front yard, but you did speak to them, and if you need outside help you can ask for it. Boundaries are about not letting people walk all over you. It's about standing up for yourself and protecting yourself from hurt. And they show others that you're confident; you care about yourself, and you're not easily broken.

Creative Exercise

Draw an image of a fence on a separate piece of paper, then hang it somewhere to remind you that it's ok to have boundaries. It's not about selfishness or being rude to people. It's just saying, "Hey, this is what I need, and I care about myself enough to get that." You will be amazed at what happens!

Conclusion

You can have boundaries in all areas. I would recommend reading more on the topic to get a good idea of where you lack boundaries and how you can really shore them up. The more boundaries you have, the greater your resilience! Because even though external forces will always be there and always out of our control, you can always find strength inside yourself. Get building!

Chapter Ten

Always Be Prepared

> *I am a free human being with an independent will.*
> —*Charlotte Bronte*

While we can't control other people, and while we can still have strong boundaries, sometimes people can still hurt us. As you begin to build confidence in yourself along with your boundaries, you need to build a sense of security as well.

Every person deserves to feel safe, and unfortunately, women are often the targets of abusive behavior. If you have been abused in the past, remember that it isn't your fault. There was nothing you did that brought about this abuse, and no one should tell you otherwise. The abuse was the choice of the abuser, and they made the decision to do what they did.

One of the ways you can build your own autonomy and sense of security is to always be prepared.

Put it into Practice

Few things feel more freeing or assuring than autonomy and safety. Sign up for a complimentary self-defense class specifically designed for women. Invest in and learn how to use pepper spray or a taser, keep a whistle on a lanyard to take with you for nighttime runs or to keep in your car, and investigate the security settings on your phone. The more you develop your own sense of security, the more confident you'll become.

This is resilience in a very physical sense, and you'll begin to believe in your own strength and ability to take care of yourself.

CREATIVE EXERCISE

Create an image that exemplifies strength for you. Is it a lotus? A fist? an eagle? Whatever it is, get it down. Add colors that also signify strength and give you courage. This image can help remind you of your own strength, both within and without.

Conclusion

You are not a victim. You are a strong, independent, resilient woman who has a will of her own. Build your own autonomy through preparation and practice.

Chapter Eleven

Be Your Own Workout Buddy

> Every girl, no matter where she lives, deserves the opportunity to develop the promise inside of her.
> —Michelle Obama

People love excuses not to exercise. Exercise is hard; it hurts, and it's easy to skip while telling ourselves, "I'll work out tomorrow." One of the best ways to keep yourself motivated is to find a workout buddy. However, that's not always an option.

If you wait until someone else is available, you may never get off the couch. Exercise is so important to your well-being, both physically and mentally, that it needs to become a priority. When you love yourself, you take care of yourself. One of those ways is through exercise.

You can be your own workout buddy, and the best part is you can exercise in any way you want to!

Put it into Practice

First off, you've got to find an exercise style you love. If you're not really sure since you're new to the whole exercise game, try experimenting with a few different styles. Spend some time online and see if you can find so many workouts for free. There are all kinds from yoga to kickboxing to dance, and you'll definitely find something that works for you.

If you want to take it up a notch, you can start going to a few classes at your local health or community center. Try out some yoga or swimming, maybe even a hip-hop class.

Once you've got the exercise you love, then it's time to start programming it into your life. Think about penning exercise into your schedule just like you would appointments or business meetings. It's a necessary part of your life, and it has to stop taking a back seat. But now that you have an exercise you love to do, it doesn't have to feel so much like a chore. Then, keep track of your progress in a journal or on a phone app so you can celebrate each milestone.

Being your own workout buddy is taking care of yourself and building yourself up. You don't need anyone else to do that. You can be that all on your own.

CREATIVE EXERCISE

Draw something on a separate piece of paper that represents your favorite kind of exercise. Is it ballet shoes? A boxing glove? Swimming goggles? Making exercise fun is the way to motivate you to do it, and when you keep this image in view, you can always remember to schedule it in!

Conclusion

Just like the fact that vegetables are good for you, there is no getting around the fact that exercise is a necessary part of life. We need to do it in whatever form it takes for us. Forget about the old traditional ways of just running or just lifting weights. Exercise can be whatever you want it to be. And as you physically build up your body, you're also building up your mind and heart.

Be Your Own Workout Buddy

Chapter Twelve

Let Go of Negativity

> "A champion is defined not by their wins but how they recover."
> —Serena Williams

Negativity can build up like an emotional plaque. If we don't deal with it, soon it's all we see when we look in the mirror. Soon the image of fire reminds us of a childhood accident with a gas stove, not a lovely campfire out in the woods. While that old scar can teach us how to avoid pain, it can also hold us back.

If you burned your hand on the stove once, does it mean all stoves are dangerous? Will you never use the stove again? Will you hold onto that pain so much so that you can't actually live your life?

That is what negativity is like. It's almost like cancer, building and growing inside of us the longer we hold onto it. But eventually, we have to sit down and realize, hey, this is not a good, happy life. All I can see are the bad things, and all I can see is stress and anger and hurt in my future.

When that happens, it's not because it's actually true. It's because you can get so used to looking at life through a negative lens, and so that's all you see. But don't worry! If you can learn to look at life through a negative lens, you can retrain yourself to look through a positive one too. It's going to hurt a little bit, but you can let go of negativity and start seeing the positives and the beauty in your life.

Put it into Practice

Do you feel like you're being held back by your negativity? Are you not as happy or as productive as you could be because of it? Try conducting this exercise. Every night for a solid week, write down every single thing you did that day from making French press coffee and running the dishwasher; to making it to work on time to sending off emails. Just get it down. This can be a pretty boring list, and that's ok. We're trying to retrain the brain here.

After that, start highlighting the things in that list that are positive. Maybe finally got to a task you've been putting off. You had patience with a frustrating coworker. You made it on time to pick up your daughter from play practice. Even those positive things you might find insignificant should be marked down! Your eyes will start to be opened to those good things in life, no matter how small. Over time, these brief moments of living in gratitude will offset the brain's negativity bias. It'll help jumpstart the journey towards letting go of your negativity. Being proud of even your smallest achievements will cultivate self-confidence and resilience which will help that negativity stay away.

CREATIVE EXERCISE

Take a separate piece of paper and draw an image that symbolizes letting go to you. Maybe it's you standing and dropping things from your hands. Whatever it is, draw the things in it that you're letting go of. Is it fear? Negativity? Hate? Anger? Keep this image close by to remind you that you need to let go of things that no longer serve you.

Conclusion

Think of negativity as excess weight on your body that's keeping you unhealthy. Only this time, it's keeping you both mentally and emotionally unhealthy. It's holding you back from finding the true joy in life that you deserve. Let go by looking through that positive lens and bring happiness to you.

Part Four: Love Your Capacity to Grow

Chapter Thirteen

Indulge in Meditation

> Be happy in the moment; that's enough.
> Each moment is all we need, not more.
> —*Mother Theresa*

It may sound counterintuitive, but growth can come with stillness and staying in the moment. Bringing our minds to the present helps to reduce the stress we have about the future. In that present state, we're not thinking about anything else. Imagine the relief you could feel! For a few minutes a day, we can just be and listen to ourselves breathe and exist. Nothing else is there to bother, judge, or stress us out.

This is meditation in action and I challenge you to indulge in it each day. I call it an indulgence because it's a beautiful time of safety, warmth, and self-love if you let it be. Meditation gives you a chance to press the pause button on life for just a few minutes if that's all you have. It lets you remember that you're human, that you need rest, and that you need the chance to remember who you are and take a moment to appreciate your presence.

Give yourself permission to have this indulgence. Breathe deep, and enjoy your own company for a little while. Let the array of thoughts pass through your mind.

Put it into Practice

Create a sensorial cocoon for yourself in your home just for meditation. It should be a place dedicated entirely to you and your thoughts, without any external distractions. Make it a safe place you love to escape to. Include whatever decorations you want which promote serenity. Download a meditation app, or bookmark guided meditations online that correspond with your mood or align with one of your goals. Maybe you want to meditate to reduce anxiety, let go of negativity, and practice gratitude. Start with a one or two-minute session, then gradually work yourself up to longer meditations.

Taking time aside to meditate can help the fog clear, and can help you focus on rest and gratitude. Indulge in meditation, and you will reap the benefits.

CREATIVE EXERCISE

Color a mandala. It is a peaceful, mindful exercise, and it's a meditation in and of itself. The intricate details of the design will focus you as you enjoy the relaxation of coloring.

Conclusion

Surely you've heard of all the benefits of meditation before, but it can feel like a real chore to put it into your day. Remember, it can happen anywhere and at any time. While having a place devoted to meditation is wonderful, it's not necessary. Squeeze it in during your work day if you need it. Just carve out some special time to just be you and let everything else pass you by.

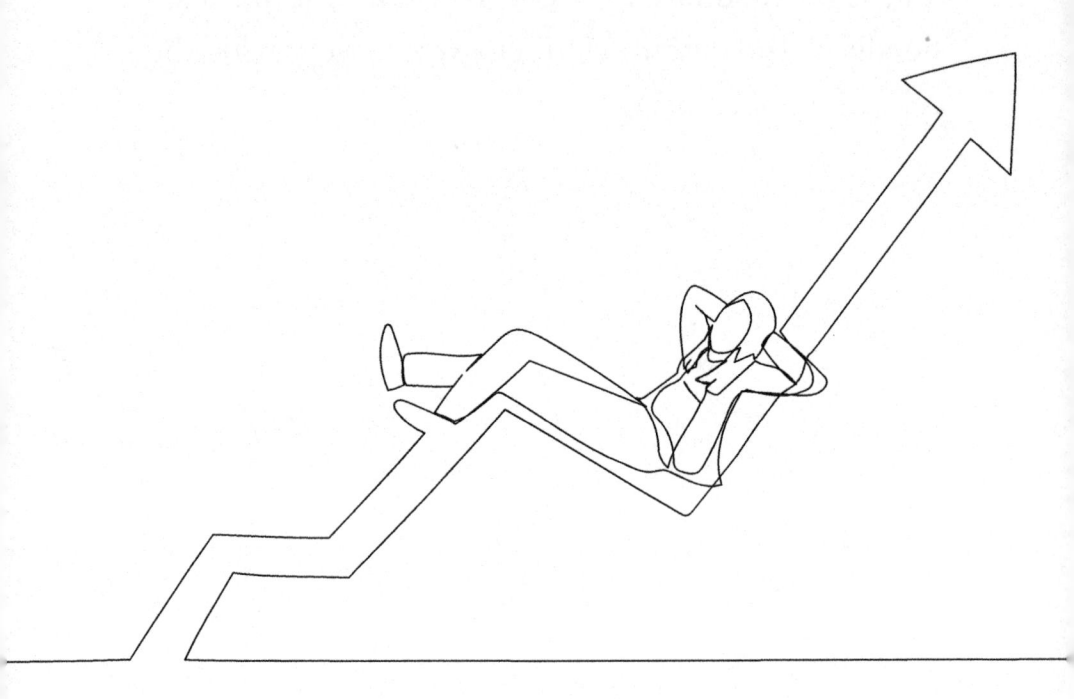

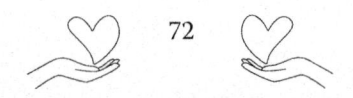

Chapter Fourteen

Grow an Incredible Garden

> Passion is the log that keeps the fire of purpose blazing.
> —Oprah Winfrey

Returning to nature is one way to find peace. In your spare time, head outside and cultivate a garden of your own. It functions as both a hobby and a mindfulness practice. Nature is a living reminder of the importance of balance. Things die but their remains nourish new life. Storms roll in, but then a time of peace comes just after.

One of the things I love about nature is that it shows me how small I am in the big picture. There is so much more going on around you in the world than the problems in your own life. It doesn't mean your problems are insignificant; it means that there is a life beyond. It can help give you perspective when you feel like negativity is taking hold of you.

PUT IT INTO PRACTICE

Set out a piece of your yard to devote to a garden. It can be a few potted herbs in your kitchen or a full makeover of your existing yard. Either can help get you outside as well as bring you the perspective that nature provides. Cultivate a garden and look for ways that it mirrors your progress as a person. The more tender loving care you give to a plant (and yourself), the more it flourishes (and so do you!).

Gardening is proven to reduce anxiety, stress, and depression (ScienceDaily, 2022). It can be a unique way to meditate and practice mindfulness. As you plan your garden, use plants that not only fit your climate but also align with characteristics you'd like to emulate. For example:

- Calla Lily: Beauty
- Blue Hyacinth: Constancy

- Ivy: Friendship
- Mint: Virtue
- Sage: Wisdom
- Tulips: Passion

Then, you can watch as your garden grows and so do you.

Rise Again

CREATIVE EXERCISE

Color an image of a garden. If you can't find one that suits you, draw your own. Be sure to add all the plants/flowers that you've included in your garden at home to mirror your growth as you progress!

Conclusion

Just spending time doing something outside of yourself is helpful. Gardening gives you a chance to push your hands into the dirt, reconnect with the earth, and remind you of what's important. It's meditative, peaceful, and gives you a chance to learn something new.

Chapter Fifteen

Fight the Good Fight

> There are two ways of spreading the light: be the candle or the mirror that reflects it.
>
> —Edith Wharton

As you begin to build your own confidence and resilience, the only natural next move is to start thinking about others. When we are able to find love for ourselves, we realize that we have so much love in ourselves to give.

In today's world, we are bombarded with causes that offer us a chance to get involved. When you find something you care about and can give time to, it makes you feel a part of a community and something bigger. It can help you build confidence in yourself. Nothing builds up a sense of self like putting others first.

Put it into Practice

Consider the causes that move you, from women's rights to providing care to those in need. Choose one that speaks to you, then volunteer your time and talents to a local nonprofit that does work you feel is important. Alternatively, keep a goodie bag in your car with items you could offer a homeless person or someone in need. These things could be a need– a pair of socks, a few nonperishable snacks, and bottled water.

The return on these efforts is priceless. You are making an effort to do the right thing even in the midst of all your busyness. It's a chance to take you outside of yourself and look at others in the world. You won't regret it.

CREATIVE EXERCISE

Draw and color an image of a hand reaching out. Through this image, you can remind yourself that you have the strength and skills to give to others.

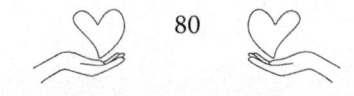

Conclusion

We all have our own problems and our own things to work through. While that takes so much time and attention, and you deserve that attention, there are other people you can reach out to as well. Build your confidence and your resilience by helping others whenever you can. Remember, even something small counts!

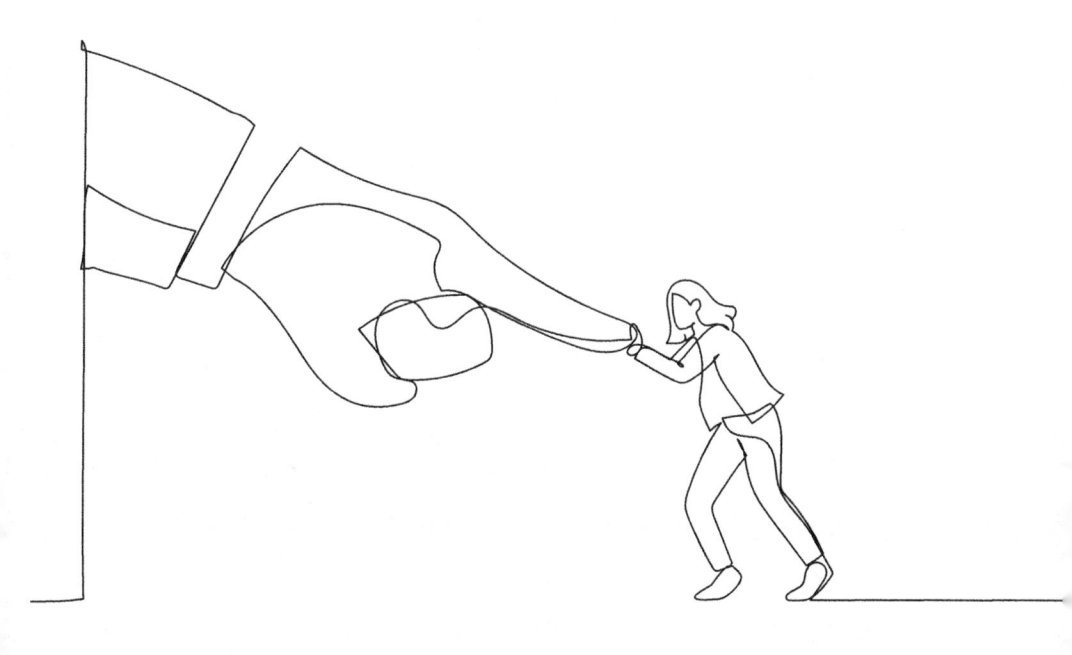

Chapter Sixteen

Inspire Yourself With Words

> "She was becoming herself and daily casting aside that fictitious self which we assume like a garment with which to appear before the world.
>
> —Kate Chopin"

Regret can affect our daily lives. We think about the past and get down on ourselves for what we did or said, thinking that if only we did something different, we'd be happier. But the present is what it is. There is no going back. All we can do is make the choices we need to make in the present moment, and try our best.

We can also try to make better choices in the future. One of the ways I like to encourage my readers is to think about inspiring their future selves. It's a way to reflect on the past, meditate on the present, and help their future selves make even better decisions. We can't change the past, but we can make adjustments in the present and work towards an even better future. There's always hope for tomorrow.

PUT IT INTO PRACTICE

Write a letter to your future self. To make things specific, write a letter to yourself ten years in the future. In this letter, I want you to write all that you've accomplished thus far (focus on the positives) and encourage your future self to work hard in the future to continue to do well.

Consider all that you've endured, and be sure to remind yourself to be grateful for what you've been through in the past. Then, write what you hope to encourage in the decade of the future self you're writing to. What are your goals and dreams? In that letter to that future you, say what you hope to accomplish even twenty or thirty years in the future.

This letter is meant to inspire your future self to keep on going even when the going gets tough.

CREATIVE EXERCISE

On a separate piece of paper, draw and color an image of a writing desk and a writing implement. Words are powerful, and we can inspire others and ourselves with words. Focus on that power as you color this image. Keep it handy so that you remember the wonderful power of words to effect change and create motivation.

Conclusion

Words have power, and they can harm or help. They can also inspire. Use what you've learned from your past and your present to help your future self. Mistakes we've made are in the past, and we can't change them. But there is always hope to have a happier, brighter future. That's one of the best things about life.

Inspire Yourself With Words

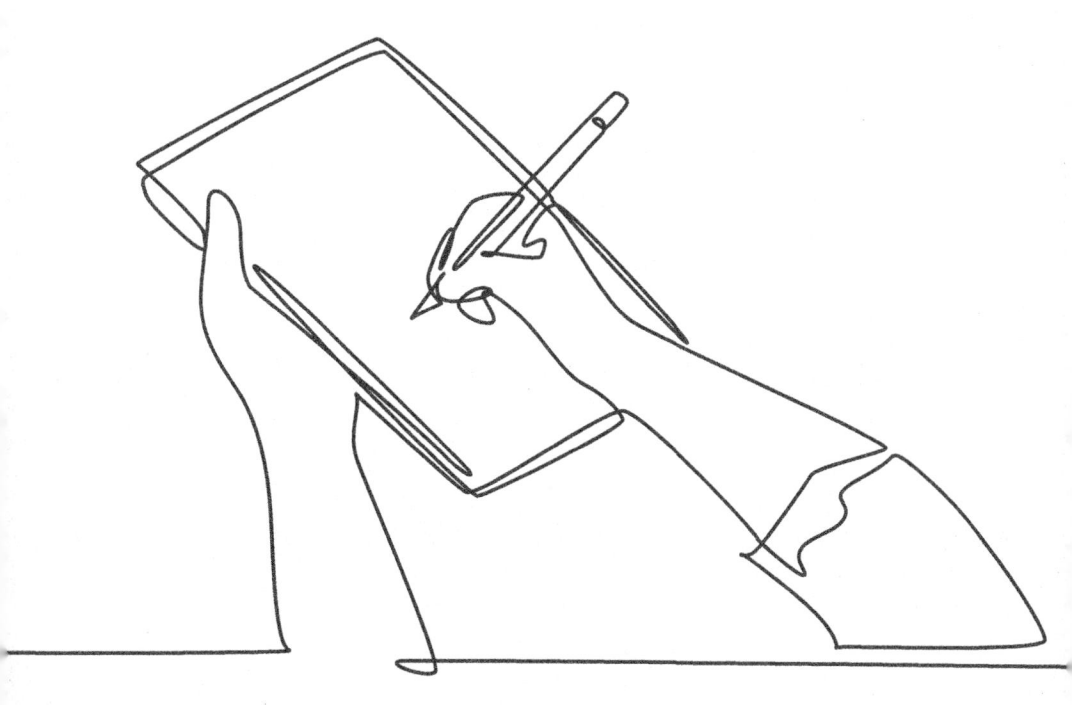

Part Five: Love Your Power

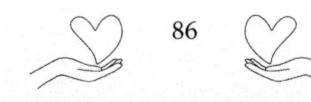

Chapter Seventeen

Anchor Yourself

> " I am not afraid of storms, for I am learning how to sail my ship.
> —*Louisa May Alcott* "

While having people in our lives is a comfort and a joy, we must also learn to depend on ourselves. We each have our own unique journey on earth, and we must be able to keep ourselves strong and centered as we go along. We have to learn to be able to lean on ourselves and turn to within ourselves for that strength needed to get through any difficulty.

I know it can be so easy to turn to others instantly when something hard comes our way, but I challenge you to start looking inside yourself as a tower of strength. Your internal tower should be a place you can turn to.

Life can be a collection of chaotic and wild storms, and we need to be our own anchor that keeps us safe and steady when the boat starts rocking. While we can depend on others, we should also be able to depend on ourselves. We are our own allies. We are the anchor to our own ships. We have the power to ground and center ourselves and do not need anyone else to do that.

Put it into Practice

Since grounding is a rather vague concept, you can create a tangible item or image to remind you to stay grounded and steady. I would recommend the use of a piece of jewelry that you will wear every day or a small object you can keep on you.

It can be a small necklace with a pendant, a ring, or even a bracelet. It doesn't matter. But you want to always have it with you so that you can touch it to remind yourself to be anchored. Take a pause and a breath and pull yourself back down to the ground when you feel all swept up in a storm.

It can be especially useful when you are feeling emotionally triggered. This grounding jewelry will help you pause and think about your next steps instead of jumping into frenzied action.

CREATIVE EXERCISE

On a separate piece of paper, draw a representation of peace and tranquility. Keep this image around so that you may always turn to it as another way to anchor yourself. Use subtle, calming colors, and remind yourself that peace is possible to find. We do not always have to get caught up in chaos.

Conclusion

We do not always have to get caught up in chaos. We can depend upon ourselves to find groundedness and centering. All you have to do is learn to be your own anchor, and when that next storm comes, you'll be more resilient than ever.

Chapter Eighteen
Love Your Look

> "You're always with yourself, so you might as well enjoy your company.
> —*Diane von Furstenberg*"

Loving who you are means appreciating your personality traits, but it's also about accepting and loving your body and how you look. Sure, it's great fun to dress up and try new cosmetics, seeing what all kinds of looks you can have. But that can be expensive and distracting; it hides you away from yourself.

To come to truly love yourself, you should learn to love what you've already got without any help. For better or for worse, this is what you've been given. It also helps you to focus on the positive aspects of yourself instead of what you dislike. It gets you thinking more on the path of gratitude than negativity.

And when you love yourself and appreciate your look and your body, people can see that. Your confidence and self-appreciation shine out through you, making you even more beautiful.

Put it into Practice

One way to start loving how you look is to look at yourself with no barriers, no disguises. Take a picture of your fresh, clean face—without a hint of makeup—to shift your perspective on what constitutes your version of beauty. Remember that you get to decide how you see yourself, no one else does. Even if you do not find yourself beautiful, you can still love yourself and appreciate what you have. This is you, all you, and it makes you special and unique.

CREATIVE EXERCISE

Draw a picture of your reflection in a mirror. Let it remind you that your own reflection is a part of you. It is not something to hate or to fear but to love.

Conclusion

We may enjoy many things about ourselves, but women often forget to start loving the look of their own face or body. Take the time to see yourself unveiled and learn to appreciate what you have!

Chapter Nineteen

List Your Strengths

> "Stick to your true north—build greatness for the long term.
> —Ruth Porat"

We all have strength, and even if we can't see it, it lies within us, waiting to be recognized and set free. The simple fact that you're here today, having achieved all that's come before, shows the strength in you. Life is tough, and it can get everyone down at times. But when you have the strength to keep going, that shows character and resilience.

Find your internal reinforcements and remember that these are yours and yours alone. It's very nice to receive compliments from others about your gifts, but you also need to notice and find your strengths. Even if you think you have none or that you can't find them, you can. They're inside you, you simply need to look for them.

When you focus on your strengths and seek them out, you are just working on another way to look at life through a positive lens. You are searching for the good things, the bright spots, and the more you do that, the more you will begin to naturally see them in your life.

PUT IT INTO PRACTICE

Instead of just doing a basic list, build a resume for yourself that has nothing to do with your job qualifications. Start creating a resume based on the strengths you have in the way you approach life. Think of it as you're applying for a job based solely on your life skills and positive personality traits.

If you need some help, take an online survey about your traits and strengths to see if it can spark some inspiration in you. Then ask your friends and family to provide you with one leading character trait that is a strength.

Write up your CV of personal triumphs as if you wanted to send it in for a job. Keep it for yourself and look at it whenever you feel your confidence starting to slip.

CREATIVE EXERCISE

Using different colors, write down and illustrate five of the strengths from your resume. Display them how you like and how you see them. The colors should remind you of power, strength, and skill.

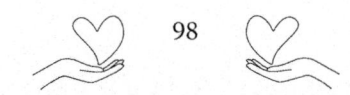

Conclusion

We all need a boost now and again as well as a reminder that we've got good stuff to give. Don't wait around for other people to give you compliments about your strengths. Do it for yourself!

Chapter Twenty

Give Yourself More Physical Space

> "Imagine yourself living in a space that only contains things that spark joy.
> —Marie Kondo"

As life goes on, we begin to build and build things around us. These can be physical things, people, social events, or work obligations. Things build and grow, and help us realize that our lives are so over-cluttered with stuff that we do not even have the space to breathe.

You may not even realize it. However, a lot of stress and anxiety can come from all the things around us, weighing on us, and taking energy from us. What we have built shows a lot about us, and it doesn't mean they are all bad or negative things. But take some time to reflect on what you have going on, and what you can finally let go of.

You will be able to breathe easier the more space you have in your life. When you have more physical space, you have time to start loving yourself the way you deserve. You have time to reflect on your strengths and gifts as well as time to restore energy to yourself that was once lost. You can create a refreshed life with more vigor in it than ever before. You will grow stronger, happier, and feel safer and more grounded than you ever have before.

Put it into Practice

Conduct a deep clean of your entire life. This ranges from going through your possessions to cutting a few things from your social calendar. With your physical possessions, go through your items and keep only what brings you joy. The rest you can give away so that it can give someone else joy.

Only participate in social events that bring you happiness. This will also help you figure out who in your life brings you good things instead of sadness, anger, or toxicity.

Let go of habits that hinder your progress towards your goals. Keep track of your "master cleanse" on a spreadsheet so you can follow your progress as you move along.

Creative Exercise

Draw or create a to-do list template on a separate piece of paper or on your preferred note-taking software. Keep it handy for whenever you need to do your deep cleanse again. You can create the list however you like, adding sections based on what needs deep cleaning in your life.

Conclusion

Use the extra space you've created through this deep cleanse to make room for brighter, fresher objects, knowledge, friends, lovers, and experiences. You could have more time to date, more space for artwork, or more bandwidth to explore your spirituality.

Give Yourself More Physical Space

Whatever it is, you can finally let yourself breathe instead of getting overcrowded by all the things that make life what it is.

Final Words

Once we find our resilience, we become like trees with deep roots. We do not move with the strong currents of life's chaos. We remain strong throughout the storms, and when the storm clears, we are still there. That is true resilience.

It is not the absence of pain or difficulty, fear or anger. It is the ability to weather that storm. To stay grounded and rooted and to push through the hard times. I want you to always be able to come out on the other side. You may have a few scars, but they no longer have to be open wounds.

You are the strength, power, and light you seek. You have all the right tools to build resilience inside yourself.

You can build this precious resilience through:

- loving your **generosity**
- loving your **buoyancy**

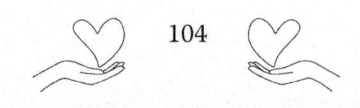

- loving your **truth**
- loving your **capacity to grow** and
- loving your **power**

You can see that the common denominator in all these tasks is love. Love is where it needs to begin. Just like when you treat a plant well, it flourishes, so do you. Treat yourself with kindness, respect, and appreciation. Show compassion for yourself; take care of yourself, and look for your strengths instead of your weaknesses.

You will blossom and shine. The strength you find through loving everything about yourself will display itself in beautiful resilience. Those storms will come, but you are strong, like a tree with deep roots. You have the power to get through anything and come out on the other side, made better and even stronger.

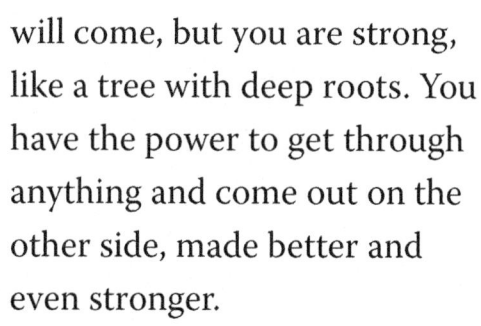

Bonuses
OUR GIFTS FOR YOU

Subscribe to our Newsletter and receive these free materials

www.specialartbooks.com/free-materials/

References

Instagram: @specialart_books
Facebook Page: Special Art Books
Website: www.specialartbooks.com

Impressum

For questions, feedback, and suggestions:

support@specialartbooks.com

Nina Madsen, Special Art

Copyright © 2023, Special Art

www.specialartbooks.com

Images by © Shutterstock

Printed in Great Britain
by Amazon